I0162121

# A Chasm
# Flight

# A Chasm Flight

123 POEMS SPANNING FOUR YEARS

*Colin Knapp*

© 2018 Colin Knapp
All rights reserved.

ISBN: 0692993819
ISBN 13: 9780692993811
Library of Congress Control Number: 2018901093
November Moon, Union, MI

# Acknowledgments

~⤴~

To ALL THE BEAUTIFUL PEOPLE in my life here and gone. To Irving, Hawthorne, Poe, Gogol, Melville, Maupassant, Chekhov, among others for their fearlessness with the short story. To all the good men and women out there fighting the good fight, whatever battle it may be. Hold ground, press onward. Enjoy.

## <u>Proem</u>

We live inside these bodies, and we must listen to them and not push them too hard or too fast, or slow them down too much with pity lest they give out on us prematurely. We all give out in the end. Whenever that is. Here is the in between. Circumstance, coincidence. Cuisine.

# Contents

# To-day

One hundred
Years ago
We wrote
Today
To-day.

Today we find
Hoodie, Selfie, and
Twerking have made
The Dictionary
Cause books
Also have
Lonely
Days

Abbreviations
Short sayings
Exclamations
Know what
I'm sayin'
Symbols
Fingers

Emojis
Text
Pics
Etc.
Yet
Just as
Readily clouds
Seem darker over
Lonely Days of Literature

The quiet serenity of a
Well-composed sentence.

These days
Everyone's
The Essence
The Rage
Legends
Rebels
Icons
Epic
Boss
Bomb
The Elite—

Can you bring back
Yesterday
For a day
Or
Half a week?

No—
Today
Will be
To-Day.

# Hang-Ups

Embarrassing
Can't side-step
This
Certain
Evil Genius
Wrapped inside
An uncertain
Past

Is a mid-life crisis
Worth the
Crash
Reinventing
Relearning
Becoming
Someone
New?

Do I have to?

Do what you do
End up chewed up

Festering on sidebars
That may or may not
Be whatever
Or even
True
No
Clue
Hunches
Up my spine
Only wanting to
Remember
The way we felt
When I made
You smile
Head calling
Me
A
Fool
Reminiscing
On a past
That will
Never
Be

Only are
Who you are
I'm only me
Two pieces
Stuck
Infinitely
Jamming
After

Lifetimes
Of
Bliss
Moving
Free

To the store!
To shop!
Time
To invest
In a
New
Top
Of the
Line puzzle?

Yes
Onward
We go
Ugh
This
Heartache's
Pretty rough
No more
Cuddles
Or
Snuggling?

How do you simply…?

# Young, Dumb &
# Full of Fun

⌒

Yep
I've
Been
Here-n
Done this
A time or three
Now I'm back ☼
For a midnight
Shopping
Spree?

Wee—

Do ya know...?
Do ya *know*...?
Do *Ya **Know**...!!!*

*Woo!*

Shoot
I just
Woke
Up.

# Why Did You Do That?

You know
I'm insecure—

Trying to make a
Jealous guy
Jealous

What the
Why?

It begins
Playfully
On the sly
I know
Innocent
Speculation
Temporary happiness
Disenchantment
Complications
Ending in

Misery
And
Regret

Unfortunately
Both sides need
Equal sides to
Hold onto I
Regret to
Inform
You

Have we forgotten?

Mutable fire's
Incapable of being
Caged
No matter how tight the
Chains
We will always slip away
In the night.

# Tempting Rational Despair

Bearing the
Burden of
Love's
True
Strain
Is
Painful
Not easy
A
Taxation
On
Pistol
Fingers
When hearts
Upon the
Sleeve
Of a
Lovesick
Weathervane

The Heart attracts what it
Wants to believe—
The Mind attracts what it
Believes it can
Conceive

Both
Achieve

Must
We
Ceaselessly
Marry these two?

Or is
Divorce
Eternal?

# Write, Right!

Ha ha *ha!*

First Saturday
Morning
In a while
Boyz & Girlz—

One cup of
Coffee
In
And
My sass
Sits in this
Chair pounding
Out pearls, slicing inked metal
Dashes-n-tight-cropping swirls against
Back-swooping slashes, black ink gnashing
Nitpicking the screen, prepping the
Excavation of this next turning
Point the following scene
Beginning and end-

Ing firmly in
Mind
As
I
…
I
…
I
…
Squirm
All you like
I don't care
Keep working
My good
Man
Stay awake
You'll be a much
Much happier
Clam.

# Worried About Things
# I Can't Change

Walking the
Outskirts of my
Rented field—
Appreciative for
Land to walk
In silence

Such beauty in the trees
Sadness drops
Quickly
I weep
Not sure
Why

Later I tell
My wife
It's not
Her

A man needs
A moment
Alone

All of us

Our
Own

Want to tell my little
Girl to laugh more
But she keeps
Sticking this
Fricking
Movie
In my
Mug
(Ironic
Huh?)

Would like to say hi
To my stepson
But he never
Looks up
From his
Game
(Me either
Once.)

Aging
Reckoning

Dissolving
Connections
Not everything
About me
Wandering
Random
Soliloquy
Bushy
Tails
Squirrels
Subtle bunnies
Changing leaves
Everything elegant
Hard to believe
Just need a chance…

Coming back
From this walk
A different
Man.

# Gulf

On the
Other side
Of the world
I feel it too—

Doesn't matter
If
It's
The
Next
Town
Over or
Down the
Avenue

I can't
Get to
You.

# EHS ½

Back in the
Day
OMG
Running laps
And laps around
The Neighborhood Track—
Beach Drive to Sheridan &
Back around to
Beach—
My
Gut
Hungry
For that
Peach of a
Record sitting
Plump-n-dormant
Since that record year
In '78
When D. Hoover
Set it straight

In the Spring of 1978
We'd just moved
Back to E-Burg
From GR—
And I was
One
And a
Half…

*~Half~*
*~Half~*
*~Half~*

*The Half Mile*
*Gut check*
*Time*
*Crushing*
*Submission*
*Sprinting*
*A run*
*Red hot track*
*Surface*
*Annihilating*
*Your buns*
*Air thin*
*Blacking out to*
*Win final*
*Death snorting*
*Grunts on*
*Failing*
*Shins*

*Of*
*Fire*
*Calf*
*Thigh*
*Shoulder*
*Lactic acid*
*Explosion*
*Overdose*
*Over &*
*Over &*
*Ahhh…*
*Why…*

Seventeen
Years later
~1995~
I set
The
800
Meters
A touch
Straighter

And in 2012—
Seventeen
Solar
Laps
Into the future—
It's changed
Hands again
I see

Congrats J.C.
J. Clark
Here's to
Another
Sweet
Seventeen.

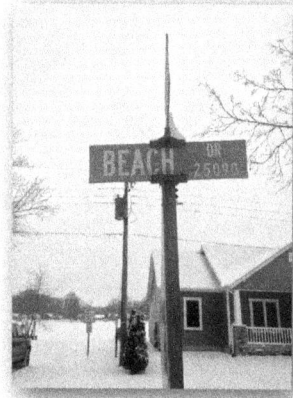

# Speechless

I tried

Trust
Lacking
Insecurity
Beat the
Life out
Of me

Beat
Me
D
 O
  W
   N
   ↓

Don't really know
What to say
Wandering
Around
Town

*I'll try*
*I'll try*
*Try*
Done *trying*

Reasons for my
Jealousy
I can't
Explain
Because
You'll say
They're no big
Thing—

I hate this

From the
Start
Deluded
Myself
Into
Thinking
There was
A chance
For us for
There was
Never
Another
You

Ran and hid
From

Myself
Too—
Closer now
Contentment
'Cause
You
Were
Correct

An unhappy life is
Simply too
Long

Neglectful
Burdensome
I believe you
It's a bitch
You've
Gone through
Disinherited love
Unacceptable pains
Misplaced trust
The pressure itch
Of a fully
Responsible
Life

Where does it go?

Can it end up
Divine?

Will we remember?

One minute
At a time
Each
Splendid
Second
This
Instant
Be present
Get it done—

What's so important?

What is it?

Say it.

# My Heart Seizes

Trying
Numb
Cold
Ice

Isolation

How can you love
Someone
So long
Only to
Discover
You've
Never
Recognized?

I've been here
Before
Haven't I?

Blue-eyed
Pixie Sprite

My stomach turns
In pain
At our
Memories
Fading
…

# Impulse

First
Instinct
Carry it
Far

Out past reservoirs
Everlasting
Spheres
Out of sight
Ever-blooming
Second thoughts
Of the night
Burned
Hesitation
Not returned
Don't consider
Participate

Showing up
Suffices
On this date

Follow our misguided notions
Our omnivorous minds
Into the deepest
Cells of our
Secret
Selfish
Selves
Harnessing
Each vital element
Not despising
What we've
Finally set
Free—

Alive
Freshly crying
Whispering torrents
Through the
Trees.

# Join Hands

Outside all the hoopla
Color-coordinated
Hidden beneath
Twinkling
Glee

I
Just
Want
You to
Know how
Grateful I am
For everything
You have
Given
Me.

# Love is Dead

In such a Contemporary Age
What
Really
Is the point?

Everyone seems
Disjointed
Disappointed
Divided these days—
Everything that once
Brought us
Together
Tears us apart
Leaves us
Alone

Terrified of the word
Goodbye
Stemming from
An initial…

Hello?

Hell no
Lost my
Heart a year
Ago

It's cumbersome
Building statues
Putting those
We love
On pedestals
And then
Have trouble
Reaching
Up
When
What
You
Finally
Find is
You.

*Me?*

The search continues…

I love my kids dearly
Yet I dearly miss
A Queen.

# Last Days of Summer

Drinking Moosehead Lager
Breezy summer day
Feeling luxury
Taking it
Easy
Realizing
Eventually
I should swing
'Round to get a hold of—

Yo yo yo – my man!
You're in Michigan
Next month?
I will see
You
Soon
Brother-man

A great day

A
Great

Day for
Reaching
Escape velocity
Of the
Mundane

One of
Those days
When the sun
Slices twinkling
Through otherworldly
Panes
Undiscovered colors
Mosey the hours
Shadows grown longer
On afternoon lawn
Electric slumber
All deeply
Honest
And
Cool

Monday
Labor Day
Nonchalance
A rule
Observed
While some
Still find
Work
Others feel
Compelled

To
Savor
Flavorful
Remains of
Summer Love
Endless Friendship
Nature's sunny best
Unending summer days
Like this one—

One I
Should have
No problem
Recollecting.

# Lift-Off

Vibrating
Turning
Gravity
Inertia
Burning
Struggling
Tire friction
Air resistance
Heavy baggage
Four souls
Physical
Emotional
Mental
Spiritual
Enough
Fuel for
The Flight
Moving quickly
Physics abide
Engine kicks
Up

Suddenly
Riding on Cushions of Sky

Invisible supports
Day's fair
Climb
Thru
Airy
Clouds
Soaring
High
Over
Pleasant
Intertwining
Streams
Down
Below
Where once
Somewhere
Once
I remember
I had dreams.

# Once Again Unknown

I need
It
Now
Power
Courage
Conviction
Volcanic grace
Intestinal fortitude
Instant assimilation
Strides forward
On my own
With
Two
Little
Ones
In tow

I ask it
Only of you—

I need to Sing
Out—

Crouch
Ready?
Spring

# If ... Then

If only you could have been
Less bossy
Renegade Lover
Let me get a word in
Once in a green moon
It'd have been
Pretty
Peachy
Keen sweet
Having a
Relationship
More than friends

Maybe we still can

Realize that one night
Didn't deepen our
Friendship
That's
On
Me

Man
I only
Wish I
Could've
Understood us
Sooner
XYZ—
We'd be at the
Coffee Shop
Eating
Buttery bagels
Sipping
Café au
Lait
Reminiscing
With of course
Our pinkies
Fully
Displayed.

# Fuck

Fuck
Oh *fuck*
What have I done?

What have I done
To the ones
I love?

# So Little Remains

In love
You
Wannabe
First and only—

Only
Doesn't
Work that
Way

Saying good-bye
Disintegrates
Large and
Minute
Part-
Icles
I
N
T
O

I-
Cic-
Les
Holes
oO°
In the
Ozone
$O_3$
So little
I take
With
Me
Thru
This life
Good bad
Indifferent
Memories
Choices
Things
Relations
Confusions
All struggling
To make sense
And to
Finally
Make it all
Right

Regardless

What was
Or
Wasn't
Has now
Taken flight.

# Remember This?

Left home when it grew dull
New circumstantial
Opportunities
Rippling across
Salty aquamarine waves
In the service of
My country

Reminisced plenty upon
Home's lush greenery
Unique
Midwestern
Synergy
As my
Ship
Steamed
Wakes
Five football fields
In length plus
Three thru

Salt
Blue
Seas

Navy first
Motorcycle trip
Later

Tried the business of
Show and pain
Theatre

Beginning to understand
A lot can't be
Planned

Snow melts back
Into rain

I'm here again?

Some
Shape
Or
Form
Remains
Regaining
New World
Purpose.

# Single Card Reading

Camping
Glastonbury
Culver Indiana
Eighty acres of
The Chicago School of
Healing Arts' Branch
Office
Theatre

That evening
Back in 2010—
After a delicious organic
Banquet in Heartwood Hall—
A simple Tarot card
Reading
One
Major
Arcana
Plucked at
Random from a
Large shiny

Aluminum
Popcorn bowl
Hinting at
Future
Fate

Oh, great
I draw
**~Death~**

Says
The High Priestess
Death is
Rebirth
Colin
It's
Change
Not bad
Good
With a
Compassionate
Nod

Looking back
Black Magic
Death was
Spot-on
Correct—
I had a
Pleasantly

Uncanny
Change
In my
Life.

# One-Upmanship

Clean-cut
Sharp suit
Eyes my
Shirt &
Tie

What's the matter?
Don't know how to
Tie
A Double Windsor?

Not sure
Mr. Taver
What is that?

Smug grin
Whispers to his
Wife
She giggles

My girlfriend shakes her head—
Says don't listen to them

Taver's got a fresh burn
Must've hit the
Tanning bed
Earlier
Like
Just
Before
We got here

Pretentious jerk

The Best Man praises
The Groom
While
The Maid of Honor declares
The Bride her
Best friend
Forever
Saying
She will
Never change
For anyone

They're young
We're even younger—
We all sense some kind of
Change

Anyway
We stand to toast
Taver continues
Boasting

And I wish
I could just…

My girlfriend slips me
An inflated
Whoopee Cushion
A *Whoopee Cushion?*
Where in the *world*
Did you get—?

Just do it!
She whispers

So…

During
The next
Communal
Laugh at some
Semi-humorous
Remark
I quickly
Slip
The
Pink
Cushion
Of
Whoop
Onto
Its
Intended
Mark.

# It's Necessary

♫
Gotta change that *booooooty*
Gotta *change* the booty
Gotta change dat
*Boooooty*
We gotta change the
*Boooooty*—

We gotta change that booty.

You got a poopy booty
Got a poopy
Boooooty
Got a
Poopy
*Boooooty*
You've got a
Poopy boooooty—

(Intermission)

Da ding*!*
You had a poopy booty.
♪

Don't you
Feel better
With a clean
Diaper
Bud?

*Gah!*

See?
Daddy
Nose.

# iGen

Gen A
Gen ZZZ
Why must
Generations
Of citizens
Be named
Suchlike
These?

Cuz it's easier
Takes less
Time—

Yeah
I know
I'm Gen X
Slime—
Generation X
From what I've read is
A lost generation

I think back to Graduation Day
June X, 1995 *(I think?)*
The days leading up—
We did seem excited
A little melancholy—
Maybe it was the
Times or maybe
It was just me
Two months
Of liberty
Family
Friends
A girl of
Beauty
I'd
Miss
Before
Diving
Into
Naval
Service
After twelve
Years of schooling—

I'd miss
Pretty much
Everyone

Gen X
Baby—
Children

Of the sun
Raised in
The 80s
Under
WWII
Korea
Vietnam
Astro music
Decent values
Drifting along
In our own
Canoes
Because
We like it that way
Because we're
Easy we're
Fun
Plus
We
Still
Get our
Shit done

Then came
The Millenials—
An interesting bunch
Of budding
Perennials
Unafraid
To love
I love

Their
Detached
View blockade
Between
The selected
Few
Forget-
Me-
Nots

Now it's iGen
Or iNation
I know no
I feel like
Robot.

# Knapper's Number

It's no Martingale
But it's
Close

A
Special
Equation
Worked out
On my
Own
Amidst
CIC watch
Umpteen million
Circling the Caribbean
In the darkest hours of
Night
Counter Drug Operations
Staring off into
Early morning
Blackness

Maybe one
Tanker
10,000 yards
Starboard
To the right
I dreamed of
Raking in
Mighty
Sums—
Blackjack
Craps
Roulette
Foxwoods
Mohegan Sun
Video poker
Baccarat
Crystal Palace
The Bahamas
Atlantis
Ecuador
Pai Gow Poker
Panama, St. Croix
St. Thomas, St. John
Curacao
San Juan
Puerto Rico—
Scoring enough moolah to
Basically party, eat, and
Sightsee for free—

Knapper's Number
Unfortunately
Had many
Many
Flaws
Unforeseen.

# One Smart Fellow

One Smart Fellow
He felt
Smart—

Say it
Five
Times
Fast.

Excuse me
Ma'am?

Don't pass
Any gas
Please

Share the brownies, though—
You're sure to get
Brownie points.

# Prepare to Forget

Brooding
Slightly moody
This Christmas Eve
Too many hidden
Fears still
Lingering
Near—
Threat Assessment
Leaving me
Hollowed
Out
And
Found

Just wondering
Do these days equal
Some kinda final
Lesson?

Something that it was
All about?

The world's still
Around after the
Return of
Quetzalcoatl
In 2012

The past is
**Present**
Is now
Again
The
*Past*

So much
Passed
Into
Prying
Prayers
Out of
Nights'
Heartaches
Alone
Hesitation
Not worth much
Dreamless
Flightless
Days overflowing
Spilling wrath
Into hot
Responsibilities
To my country and

My service mates
To my family
And to
Me?

Remember
It's not all on you

Too much time in regret
I know I should
Forget—

Forget not to work on
The proper
Way.

# Crevasse Onrush

You could
But why
Would
You?

Pull up dude
Life ain't so bad
It's over so
Quickly
Anyway

Ride it out

Well
Maybe
This
One
Rude
Particular
Interlude

Seems
Feudal
But I happen to know it gets better soon.

# Low

A
Hole
Lonesome
Long-filled w/
Someone close

Too close—

Such
Good friends
So many
Promises
My heart
Will
Always
Hurt with
Love for us

We've been through
Enough

Innocent
Loneliness

Those born
Different
Born
Before their
Time
Born older

I never expect anyone to
Stay with me

It's a
Shame
Because
We came
Together
Untied knots
Held each other
Close
In cold snow
Hot city
Summer nights
Cool farm winds
Quiet winter
Whispers
Beach sun
Warm
Gin

Prizm
Of
The
Moon
Electric
Fission
I only wanted
To love
You—

This was the hardest decision.

# A New Year

What an unexpectedly
Drastic
Turn
Of
The
Page

I'm not going anywhere

Staying rooted
Right here
Quiet
Resolute
Focus
Stately
Sage
Prepare
Thou Ark
January's dark

But it's no
Longer
Blue—

After all

It's
New Year
Number two.

# Cliché

Loses
Power
Swoop!
Dries
Crashes
Changes
Too much
Raging water
Crystallized
Activity
Frozen
Frost
Now
Lost

Slothful speech
Lazy expressivity
Extra effort
Explaining
What you
Really

Mean
Floating
Around
Half-baked
Gathering
Dust
And
Other
Particles
On your face

Sift
Settle
Yellow
Mellow man
A few extra
Seconds
Saves a fellow
Instead
Sam I am
You jive-ass turkey
Man!
Don't give no
Contribution
Clydesdales
No dental
Exams!

# Need a Bubba

Nope
Sorry Bud
Bubba's broken
U tore a hole thru the
Nipple &
Daddy's
About
Ready to
Throw this stinky
Thing out the
Window

Look at my
Bed
You don't wanna
Lay in your
Crib
Now we
Both have to sleep in
Milk

It's okay
Daddy's
Just tired
Gotta work in
Two
Hours
Breathe
Let's find
A dry spot

Teetering
On the
Edge
Of
Bed
My
One
Claim
To dry
Surface
Space his
Cries waning
When I feel warm
Little fingers tickling
My lower back—
He likes reaching out
Sometimes
Ensuring I'm still
Intact—
Oh sweet mother of
!@#$%^&*

It's getting riper!
Those aren't fingers
At all
It's off
Off completely
His diaper....

# Tired Things of Yesteryear

⌒

Baggy pants
No belt
Pounding bass
Hanging out
What'cha doin'?
Chillin'
Naw y'ain't
You're sweating
Dude dying on da
Way you dress'd
That ain't cool
That ain' chill
Lotta work
Tuggin
Dem
Draws
Up
CoN
StanT

Ly
Cruel
Unusual
Insecurity
Like so many
Authors posing
With cats on their laps
Staring off enigmatically
Into space acting
The Other Dimension
Trying to appear
Deeper than
A sheet
Of
Paper.

# Why Waste It?

Inside
State of mind
Rev it up
Listen to it
Fly
Humming
Heightened
Creative drive

Umm why
Are you
Pondering ways to
Divert yourself?

*~Check Engine~*
    Light

Don't quit surfing
Keep cutting
Forward
Dude
Six feet

Under Turf Tomorrow Yes— It's very Lewd, Mon Punch it Out If You Need to Move around Fan the flames It's not about Perfection Not right now Not today

Ready?

Same channel Similar time Progress Even something strange Such as: *The tropics were not exotic Merely out of date Trying to Imagine The Seductive Sea.*

Under
Turf
Tomorrow
Yes—
It's very
Lewd, Mon
Punch it
Out
If
You
Need to
Move around
Fan the flames
It's not about
Perfection
Not right now
Not today

I'm ready
Ready?

Same channel
Similar time
Progress
Even something strange
Such as:
*The tropics were not exotic*
*Merely out of date*
*Trying to*
*Imagine*
*The Seductive Sea.*

# Self-Pleasure Hath
# Saved Many a Soul

There you squirm
Scattered across
The floor
Writhing
All over the bed

Better off
Disappointed
Than
Jealous
Or
Dead or
Uncertainly
Broken up on
The Rocks of Expectant
Creek w/no
Oar—

Not your finest moment
For sure
No coins in the money
Purse

Eh—
Could be worse.

# Never Again to Marry

Never again I say
Never again
This time
I say
Never do

If this never
Turns out
Cleverer
Than
Most
Then
Maybe
Just maybe
I Do?

# The Old Homestead

Hand-hewn beam
In the basement

How long you
Been there?

1865?

Final year of
The Civil
Fight?

Must've been standing
Tall and strong
Long
Before
Tree of lore
Toppled
Nearby surely as
Construction commenced
No FedEx or UPS
In them days

Delivering supplies
Only the Pony Express?

The Old Homestead
Erected near an
Old horse trail
Into town
Down to the
Railroad tracks
To pick up supplies
A horse and wagon
Path that became
Rural Route 2
Is now
M-62.

Old Farmhouse
Smelling surreal
I remember visiting
Grandma and Grandpa
M—
When I was a
Young squeal
Stepping inside
Discovering
Certain
Nooks
Cupboards
Places
To
Hide

A place
Uniquely
Inside my
Memory

Outside
Farm
Tractor
Equipment
Implements
Intriguing
Old white barn
Fifteen acre field
Chew Mail Pouch Tobacco
Advertisement now
Covered over
With
Aluminum
Side

Over and over
So much work!
Whenever we'd
Visit
We'd get it all done
*Finally*
Then we'd have
Fun
'Less there was
More to be
Done

Digging around in the soil
We still find old glass
Iron nails
Gears
Scrap
Metal
Screws
Ancient
Artifacts
Buried deep
Sleeping memories
Whispering lives
Here before
Our own

Now
More than
Ever
I am not young!
I proclaim with
Short-sighted
Disdain

Tossed out upon
The
Road
A traveler
On the open
Plain
Eating rolling tumbleweed
Pie

Seeing a Farmhouse
On the
Distant
Horizon
Always a
Satisfying sight—

One
Never spoken
Only written.

# mine, Mine, MINE

~⌒~

Get the social fix
Of the
Universe!
~U.H.B.~
Ultimate Human Being
Make dreams
Unimaginable
Come to
Reasonable
Belief!

You **NEED** this!
Bargain?
Heck—
This is YOU!

It's true true true!
Click -HERE-
Hurry you'll
Miss our special deals
The time of your life

The time of
*All* lives
Extra lives
Things to do—
Your entire world
Brought
On
Wheels
Straight
To you
No worries
Just give us
Everything
You

Can't score
Big 'less you
Invest with the
Best—
Do it now
Wow
You call yourself
A consumer?

Smell the coffee burning
Babycakes &
Then buy a
Case

It's the
Latest

Of the few
Brand new YOU!
Anyone who's *anyone*
Has
At least
Twenty-two
Thousand
Small
Little
Implant
Unnoticeable
Won't even remember
It's *you*
ALL THIS
For the extremely
Low price of
799.95
With a
Life long
Semi-binding
Contract
You bank accounts
Routing numbers
Blood stool
Samples
Little
SSN
DNA
Details
House rules
(Ya don't say?)

Hooked in completely
Completely hooked up
You'll sleep with everyone else
Own every single house
In town
Won't even have to
Wake up, dude
Hit the snooze!
Relax Mommasita
You'll never have to
Work or
Worry
Again
We're all doing it
See?
This message is a
Recording

Wanna be cool
Or a doof?

OK loser
Wait—
You're *in?*
My friend!
No time to waste!

A limo's waiting
Out front
We'll start you
Post haste.

# Nothing is Easy

Explorer's wheel bearing
Fails
More and more
Bills
Details
Life piling up
My job still not paying enough—

Alone
I sit
Penning
Remembrance

Here is here
Gone is over there
Somewhere

Why all this stuff?

Making peace with the past
Reconciling karmic debts
Still isn't enough.

# A Special Misery

Thief of my secret
Inner
Chamber
You rocked my
World for a
While
Had me
Pocketed in a
Beautiful
Snatch & grab
Robbery
With few
Remainders
Look at us
Pathetic
Resisting
Arrest

We were
Young
Strong

Destiny
Greatness
Took different
Paths thru our various
Lives—

I always
Wondered
What happened
To you—

Been a long time

Now you wish I had
Never contacted you?

Despite our end
Accept this
Mirror—
Don't barricade
Yourself
Behind
Your fears
Babe
If they said it
Then it says
A lot about
Twos &
Threes

Be confident
Be unequaled
Stay first

Do I regret it?
No
Even though you hate me
So.

Now
You say
You don't?

Yes, no, yes, no, yes, no....

# The Delicate Mallet

⌒

S
W
O
O
S
H
!
P
O
O
F
!
A
Foggy
Cloud Of
Inspirational Water Vapor
[Waterproof Watermelon]
A-Top Your Sleepy Head

# Damn

Yes you
Went there
You son of
A
Bleep

Why'd you do it?

Why'd you
Heed all
That
Sleaze?

Ugh
Forget it
I hope I can
Please
Remember
Never
Do it
Again.

# Michiana Memories

It was the toughest of times
It was the strangest of
Chimes
Tingling in the
Changing winds…

"Hey, my aunt is single."

What do you like on your
Polito's Pizza?
I'm fine with
Just my
Sausage
Ha!
I know you are

Showed me the score
#24
Returned a long lost
Feeling of
Man

Out of the darkness
Holding quietly
Your hand
Making
Me
Laugh
With
Your
Lays
Your
Coors
Your
Absolut
Grape Phillies
Hazelnut Coffee
What-the-whaaaaat?!

Everybody talks but
Remember
It started with a
Whisper

Beutter Battell Merrifield
Kamm Island
The Linebacker
Between the Buns
Bill's Steakhouse
Mr. G's
Dang girl
So many wonderful
Sistas and brothas

Family & friends
Super
Keen

I will always remember
Your laughs
Your tricks
Your beguiling charm
That insinuating
Smile
That
Smothered
So much pain
Replacing it with
Bright sun-strewn
Days of
Youth

Helping me laugh again

In the end
I just want
To say thank
You.

# Permission

Feel free to
Think what
You want
About
Me—

Thanks I will—

Whoever speaks
Next is the
Fool on
The
Hill.

# Sales Calls

Really
*Really?*
**What the f--?!**

I know you're
Trying to make a
Living—

I know
I know
I know

It's
Not you
It's your smarmy
Little company—
Not all of them
Just the greedy mercenary
Snatching small beans
Nursing insecure egos
Against everyone

No choice but to
Make you do this
We have little
Choice either
Having to
Work like
Beavers

It's not
You
It's that
Little
Robo-
Telephone
That keeps
Ringing my
Ears with
Nothing
I want to
Hear

Turn down the freaking
Volume on the
Commercials
Will ya!

Money makes the world turn
True enough I say
Although
I'd lay a
Bet

Earth and Time
Spin
Regardless
Of the Asking Price

We're all just sitting down to
Dinner
After a long stressful
Day
The phone rings
Driving us
Further
Into
Our
Plates
Because
We want it
We need it and
Because if it wasn't
Money
It
Would
Be something
Else

Head of Sales
Retail Store
Prez of a
Stifling
Factory
Floor
Hedging

Managers
Keeping their
Eyes narrowed
On bottom lines
Squeezing them
Pinching us
Greedy smiles
Dripping jowls
Howling
Howls
We work harder
Yet rarely a
Dime
It's their time
But listen to the
Subtext
Behind their
Smiling
Sales
Pitch
As
Many
Seem
Prepped
To graduate
Grade school
Ethics in
Relentless pursuit
Additional numbers
To show
Everyone
How wrong they were

About the sum of their
Character when
No one
Really Cares
Anymore

Turn down
Their offers
Watch their
Smiles wither
Away
Dollar sign
Precision
Till they
Own it
All
Today—

If not
What else?

# Do I Have To?

Yes!
I want to be your
Social media friend
Just can't remember
My
Login access
My password
All that
Tail spin

I love hating these
Invisible gates
Can't u just
Let me in?

No
Wait!
Never
Mind
Trojan
Horse

Pop-up
Spam-a-lot
Unblocked
Cookies
Nightmare
Fine
Damn you
Thanks a lot
*Ahhhhh—!*
What kind of
A.I.
Social
Nut
House
World
Do we thrive
In?

Makes real and artificial
Enemies feel like
Friends.

# Ooo

Out here in the
Exosphere
Feeling mighty divine—

What are you doing
So far up?

Feeling nearer &
Dearer
Sweetheart
Sublime

Oh—
In that case
Hi!

# Obviousness

Born with a
Titanium spoon
Nothing to work
For
No one to swoon
Still can't
Bargain with
What's real
So you turn
Into a
Drama
Grifting
Buffoon
Striking
Exorbitant
Prices
For the thrill
Of grazing
The till
Keeping the
Spree alive

Riding for
Free

It's all about your self-proclaimed
Legacy
When it should have been
About us
Mainly

Why save us when
We're shallower
Simpler
More
(Insert phrase)
Than we've
Been in
Forever?

Our
Collective
De-evolution
Nearly complete
Could be so funny
If the farce warn't
So cheap
Laugh it up
Swell
Whichever way's
Hell
All pretty
Lowbrow these

Days
Anyways
Re-shooting old
Family TV
Dramas
As
X-rated Kids' Shows
In the Bahamas.

# Writing Redux

Writing in the
Bedroom
My grandparents
Once slept
Many turns ago
Feeling the
Presence
Indescribable
Essence
Old wood
Brick
Pine
Composing
Composting
One
Word
At
A
Time ~

The most righteous thing
Going
Inspired torture
Rhyme ~

The rest?
Relaxation?

Noisy conversation.

# What Was I Thinking?

What was I
Thinking
Of
The moment
Before
You
Called?

What was it
I said to myself
Never to
Forget
Before
Love
Black-balled me into
A carnivorous
Space cadet?

# Lure of the Sea

Cast a passionate hook
Deeply
Tempting
Groundswells
Pulling fluids
Romantically
Thru your
Liquid
Baptism
That once
Belonged to
Arielle
Now
Your dreams
Won't let
You
Be
Hills of joy
Swelling heaps
Laughing
Right out loud

Out of sight
Out of
Land
Toward
Distant surf—

You belong to
*All* others—
Ambassador
Of the
Earth.

# Under a Strange
# Purple Sky

The new makes itself
Unknown
Eventually—

Is
The
Effort
Worth the
Expenditure ~
Brand new adventure?

Crows
Blue Jays
Lawn mowers
Grass clippings
Sheets of
Green
New cravings
Something new

Unexplained
Unexpected
Unforeseen
In a long
Forgotten
Time

It's what's for
Dinner

No longer
Blind
I
See

Intense Lavender
Purple Supreme

Boredom & Routine?
Not in the least

That's royalty.

# Extroverted Introvert

You're never happier
Working with
Others yet
You tend
To work
Alone

Your
Powerful mind
Your empathy for
Others are what
Others find
Attractive

How do you make
Certain they're
The
Most
Important
Person in the
School
Room?

We are not always
First glance
Or
Long
Trance

Outgoing
Before others
Get to know
Us

Never
Meeting a
Stranger
An
Ironic
Mask
Conceals a
Sensitive &
Concerned
Lass.

# Saturn in Leo

Born w/
Saturn in Leo
Sun sign in Sag
When Saturn returns
In one's natal chart
He drops off a
Disciplinary
Badge

2015
2016
It's been
True enough
For this
Sag

Allegedly
Saturn doesn't
Drag us thru
Swamps
We're not

Able to
Fully traverse
On our own

<u>Allegedly</u>.

So far Taskmaster
Saturn has
Thoroughly
Smashed me to
Louisville &
Brazil
Just
For
Kicks
And I know
He can always get

I
L
L
E
R

Ain't messing around—
They don't call me a winner
For nothing, however
So I'm keeping my
Head down.

# Pretentious Half

Some of these music groups
These days
Man
I guess
I just don't
Dig it

Rehashed spectacle
What's already
Been done
More
Legit
IMO

So little in radio land
I would actually
Get into
Buy
Put an
Album
On

Oh
Honey
Come on
It's all online
Underground
Anymore—
No one buys CDs
Tapes, or albums
Anymore
Anyhow

Fine
Still boggles
My mind
People grooving
To these
Automated tunes
I wanna say
Hey
Come on
Now
Really
Seriously
Tell me now
Does this
Really
Do it for
You?

*Really?*

Completely
Flawlessly untrue
Star-struck fan-artists
Mugging for the
Carpet crew
Cameras
Auto-tuned
All about the voice
So watch us on
TV
Right?

*Put your hands together!*
*Get 'em up!*
*Show some love!*

*Please*
Shut up!
It's a
Concert
I paid YOU
To entertain ME
I'll clap if your song's
Good enough
Till then—

Never mind
Gimme my
Money
I'm going to sleep

Shouldn't let
Those creeps
Behind the
Screens
Tell you
What's
Going to
Sell—
Dragging your
Heart thru
Hell—
They've got
The green
But
We're
The hungry
Mouths to feed

Get creative
Still believe

This trite NFL
Halftime
Show
Yeah
It was
Satisfactory
I suppose and
Utterly already gone

As the ball
Dropped
This
New Year's Eve
All I could think was
No one has any
O O
Anymore
Nothing to
Believe
*Everything*
A ratings score
Show no remorse
Doin' it for the
Almighty
Dough of
Course
Of
Course!
Thumbs
Up!
Like us @
One Million
Two **Billion**
**THREE *TRILLION*...**

Yawns
Shucks
This new
View
Kinda
Sux.

# Even Lower

Tired
Don't want
It any longer—

If we don't fight
We don't go
On

Give up on me…

That's
Too easy

I have things
Left to
Offer

One
Thing's
For certain

I'm devastated

Me too

*Don't read those…*
*You won't understand…*

That's true—
Nothing
Left to
Understand.

# Glass Soul Intermission

Mirror mirror on my
Driver's side
Visor
Will
My
Spirit
Rise into
Anything wise?

Or is my life
Simply an
Exercise
In what
Not to
Do?

An incidental
Geyser?

Voice answers
My real question

Fine

So what
In God's name
Do
I
Do now?

Surely you
Jest?

Is this normal?

I don't know
What
Is.

# Old & New Again

Down on Old Creek Road
Out by the lake
Tales unfold
Evening sky
Awakes

Warm friends
Hot sparks
Cold cider
Cool night air
Classic tunes
Midnight rare

Remember…?
So long
Ago?

How much more?
So much more!
So much *less*
We knew

Back
Then
And
Now
Even less
Regardless
Excellence to
You old friend
Help me get through
This
I'll help you over it
In the end

No need
Brother-man
Shining
Grand in
Your
Eyes
I see
Cotton
Candy
Covered
Candor
Grandeur
Upon
Most
Pies
Come on
We're running
Behind

Huh?
Hurry up
Why?
Late late late
What's at
Stake?

A party
The Party
*The Party* of the *Century*
Awaits!

# Business Cards

I have no idea where
This relationship
Stands

Few
Clues
Into
Who
I am

A
Meager
Weekly
Wage

Lunatic
Life
Approaching
Critical
Insane

Can't think
Can't write
Can't see
Too
Straight

I guess
I'll order some
New Business
Cards today.

# U-N-Me-R-Fine

True
Enough
On your end
Honey bunny
Bear

I have yet to
Release this
Demon
From
My head
My heart
Any hair
That's
Left

Didn't feel right
By the end
You know what
I mean
Not scared
Only

Searching
For me in your
World
And
As usual
In
Too
Deep

Lots of family drama
Friends in chains
Misconstrued
Womanly
Remains
Not to
Mention
The persistently announced
Theatre of the Absurd
Between
Us

Secrets.
I love you.
Don't worry.
We have time.

How many
Hours?

Understand
I cannot remain
Jealous

On the darkside
Confused
Not knowing
If you care
Light a torch
So
I
Can
Choose
Before things
In the cockpit
Start flying
Loose

Grow up!
Accept responsibility!

Honey
I've been
Through plenty
This
That and
Then some
Before

But
I've got
Someone else
I'm fighting for.

# Fun is Grand

Fun is so
Grand!

Stand up
Sarcastic
Man—

We
Still
Have
Tons of
Fun to accomplish.

# Categories & Labels

They defeat us
When we're
Looking
For
Protection
And a
Way to
Fit
In

We lose
Our credibility
Our ability to
Choose
Who
We are
To defend
Ourselves as
No one else
Can—

Our own way

At
Most
Labels
Contain
One human
Being—

Categories maybe
Three?

Tired
It takes time
We're busy
Busy
Busy
!!
Just
Don't
Forget
What it
Could be.

# Inspired Desperation

Have to get up
Do this—

What else do I
Got?

Zero
Zilch
Nada
Not

Nowhere to
Run
Everyone to
Escape
Stuck
In the mud
Coming
Undone

Don't even care

Notice
How our
Day is
Begun?

# And We're Done

Think we could've
Gotten along
Fine if
We'd
Have
Gotten
Along
In time

For all the
Rushing
Exciting
Run
It
Is
All
Done

Sad
Although

I can breathe
My heart gasps
Like goldfish
Out of
Bowls

Look at
Yourself
Once more
Those
Golden eyes
Of self-control
Believe
I'm not interested in
What everyone else has
They're imprisoned
I'm intrigued
In what you
Have—
Not what we can
Get
What we can
Offer
Each other
Unseen—

Even so
We think
Differently
Indifferently

Different values
Dissimilar interests

Maybe
This is for
The best?

# Forty

Forty and sporty
Forty and
Ugh

Simplify
Bud
Find a most
Direct route to
Happiness

What's that?

Ridding yourself
Of these toxic
Acquaintances
Making each
Day count
Snow
Rain
Shine
Radiate

Each one
With meaning
A *bit* of pride
Wake with joy
Work your plan
Plan your day
Adjust
Blaze onward
Carrying on
Smartly
With
Your
Salty
Way.

# A Day Off With Pay

Sleep in
Says the Prez
Nod and a wink
Take tomorrow off—
Slept with your mother
Last night he thinks
Smiling at the
Kid—
Mike Carew
Routing Department—
The Winner of the
Monthly Day-Off
Raffle
Drawing
Before the
Drawing even
Drew

Chief of Operations'
Main Operation
Was operating

On the
Prez
Under
His desk
No one knew
Opportunity genius
Dropping to her knees
In the Storm Shelter lavatory

These tiny
Glitches
In our—

Lemony Crickets!
I think to myself
I didn't even
Have to
Buy a ticket

I already did
Of course
Sum-Bi†©╫

# Friends and Relations

Friendships seem
Forever—
Relationships
However
Keep
Finding the ground
In
Flames

(Have you read through
Some of your own
Poems, Matey?)

No
That
Isn't it
(I don't think )
Intimacy hasn't ruined
Anything
I feel

Not a foolish clown
Nor am I bitter
With anyone's
Frown

Are my
Waypoints
Turned
Around?

My heart
Only big enough
For smaller
Payloads?

Then
Again
I checked
And I've gotten
Along with most
Everyone I've met
Along the
Road

Long as I kept my head.

# Yeah, Probably

Afterlife might prove a
Real bitch
When
You
Knowingly
Pitch yourself into
The stomach of
Corrupted Jonah
The Sailor's Devil
David Jones's
Barnacled
Cabana

Well
Rock Star
You've come
To the right place

Here we waste
No time
No effort

(Not on my part)
No face—

Here
You know
What you're
In for
Ace.

# One and One is Four

I'm not signing a pact
With
Anyone
Only trying
To help
Everyone
Along
Myself
&
My
Two
Kiddies
First

One and one is
Four

If I'm kinda
Meh
And you're kinda
Bleh

Then together
Couldn't we
Up the
Score?

# Christmas 2016

A new moon
A new groove
New moods of
Passionate
Glamour
For
These
Fabulous
Appetizing
Holidays

Home *is* where
The heart
*Is*

Vanish
Stale sorrows
A bevy of tomorrows
Replenished
Bursting forth
Red & Green

Supernovae
Confident in our
Uncertainty
Whilst
Gifts
Adorn
Twinkling
Evergreens

Bright young moons
Bloom old love
Great
Gingerbread
And
Candy cane
Potential
What else
'Cept
Under the
Mistletoe?

# Law's Always a
# Step Behind

A compliment—

What you give when
One passes
You by

No lights

A ladle pouring
Free soup
Into your
Bowl
Doesn't taste right?

Hurts
Not to know
About the
After
Show

It's lovely
To talk
About
But
In
The
End
Doesn't
Solve much
Kneeling
Before
That which
Dominates you
Locking yourself
Down
In
Imprisoned
States of mind

Accomplishments
At times
Generate
Regrets
Things no longer
Able to get
Nothing fails
Like success
Watch it
Do you
Already
Eleven miles per

Hour
Over
The Speed
Limit
You
Rebel
You.

# Soaring on Native Tongues

A dubious thrashing
A dubious man
Trashing our
Country's
Slogan
With:
Land of the Creep
Home of the Knave

Neglectful
They said
Reckless
Retiring
Rueful

I'm tired of
Breaking
News—

I want
Breaking
Diversion

Lips on
Grips on
Motorcycle trips
Saddle tongues
Loads of fun
Bustling galleries
Silvery gold-speckled
Paint guns
Kewpie Dolls
Falling open
Sledgehammer
Dings
Ferris wheel
Wings
Bam*!*
Ka-Pow*!*
Wait—
Oh
Believe me,
I'm not
Done
With a
Thing

# Confidently Cocky

What?
You think
You're the
Cat's pajamas?

And then some

Fire and Brimstone!
Laced your loins
With all of
Those?!

Two hundred and five
Fantasies
I laughed

Am I dreaming?

I don't think I understood
The question—

Wait
You're—?

# Cinema Nouveau

The first
Motion picture
May have been made
In 1889—
Thanks to Edison
Muybridge &
The Lumiere Bros—
However I believe
Cinema really began in
1897...

I know
I was there
Thank heavens.

The first film studios
Were born that year—
Joseph Frank Keaton &
Sir Charles Spencer Chaplin—
Children of the
Gay '90s

Were also
Becoming
Enticed

Until 1927
All moving pictures
Were made (MOS)
Without
Sound

Afterward
Pictures
Moving
With
Audio
Infusion
Became known
As Talkies

Ironic how
We now
Classify
Those
First
Films
As
Silent

Today
Not silent
Blockbusters

Are about as
Exciting as
Watching
Someone
Play a
Video
Game

Great fun for some—
Best movie ever
For others.

# Relationships Are Clouds

Laughing madness
Rueful gladness
Undulating
Utter fun
What
Seems to be
The
Matter with
Me?

A
Tickle
Sneak attack?

What?

Complete with
Laughs?

Morphing
Into

Gorgeous
Elsewheres
Arm
Under
Bosom
Under
Sleeve
Everyone's
Dated
These days

Everyone?
No one—
Everyone
Except
This
*New*
One

Yes
Yes
*Oh* yes
*The*
One!

*Now*—
How
Will
This
Turn
Out
?

# Thank Zeus for Cruise Control

Please
Tell me
When I wake up
In the morning this will
All have been a
Dream

*Set it at*
*Fifty-five—*
*One less thing*

A terrible dream

*Close one*
*Eye*

That
I'm home

Safely already
In bed

To Hades with
Drink.

# Liquid Courage

Can't stand up
For me
Can't stand up
To you

Another Dirty Martini—
Bourbon Whiskey
Now it's
Growing

How I used to
Appreciate
You
Brew-ha-ha
Ginny gin
Gin
Wine
The Winter of
Our Discontent
Has arrived—

No longer are
You doing
What you
Did

I'm no longer
As caring

Is this a situational
Test?

Perhaps
But I don't
Think
So

I remember
Those
Times
You popping up
In the picture
Unannounced
Undressed
Like
Boom!
There you were
A beer
A pint
A bottle
Of wine

Yes
Sorry
Sweetie
I'm calling
You out
For a
Shot
Of
Moonshine

Stay calm
Be rational
Will ya?
See the inside
Fairy tale
Fray
Realistically
From the outside
Under its stinking
Influence
Mounting debts
Fatter-n-feeling
Worse
Can't retire
Spent all my
Money
Need a nurse—

I don't know
It's

Just
Not that
Much fun
Anymore—

Besides
I get so tired.

# The Times

When taken into custody
Relax
Meditate
For it's you arresting
You

Black and white
Smite or
Spite
We still can't
Live each others'
Lives for each
Other

Must
Govern
Yourself
Or remain a
Sulking knave
Easily forgetting

Others are dreaming
Working hard every day
Gaining every
Available
Competitive
Advantage

'Tis the way
The only
Way
Between
Debt
&
Pay

The
Real rub
We all desire
Recognition
From the
Others
In the
Club
When
There's
Never enough
Love in the world

Can't you help us?

Notice
Instead
Fireworks
In the
Summer
Breeze
I can only
Think to say
Before I
Sneeze—
Remember
What it was
Like
Hearing
The flash
Seeing
The bang
For the first
Time

An entirely new
Scene

Or how about
Reining in all those
Beautiful people
I smile
Spreading powerful
Feelings of nurture

For the powerless
In this
Conscious
Self-made
World

Feel
Fortunate
Yourself to
Simply realize.

# Robert Pine's Lowenbraü

Remember when
Commercials
Used to be
Painless?

Abnormal
Strolls down
Memory
Lane
YouTube
Self-Induced
Makes me glad
I grew up
In the
80s

Watching
The Vietnam
Hippie Generation
Merging with the Millenials
The Ultimate Objectivists

Already bored with everything
Has been interesting
Now that the
Greatest Generation
Are taking their
Final
Leave—

Everything seems
So short and
Sweet.

# Creative Destruction

Paths for
Growth are
Sometimes concealed
Needing clearing
Away

I
Never
Mean to
Fly off the
Handle with
You
Babe—

We dissolve things
Sometimes to
Evolve

Some
Subtle
Some fraught
With higher

Resolve
Striving
For
Clearer
Spaces
In the
Mind
To
Find
Or cut trails
Unobstructed
Through the
Forests
Of
Time

If only to
Love
And
To be
Adored.

# Strain

My cupcake is giving me
A tummy ache

My baby girl's
Swirling me
In eddy
Twirls

Then again

What's love
Without a
Coconut
Cherry
Fritter
In the
Kisser?

If it's
Painless
I become
Anxious.

# Yel-Low

Yellow is my
Favorite color, he says.

It's a good color
Says Grandma—
It's sunny, it's friendly, it's warm

Yeah, he says
It's my best
Friend.

# Beginning to Heal

Only are
Who we are—
Take a moment of
Quiet

Listen
Begin to believe
Tomorrow
Is a
Different
To-day

You are free
Free to decide
To name new paths
To infuriate
Those who
Spend
Their
Time
Assigning

Your
Day

Do you—
Create
Untaken

Cry
Yourself
Short of
Bamboozlement

Soon
You will begin
Healing
From a painful
Emotional
Breaking
Away
That
Was
Necessary
To regenerate
Positive energy
Recreate
One muscle
Stretching
Smile
At a
Time

As
The
Clock
Keeps
Ticking
Forward as
We all should
Embracing small
Victories on
Our private
Journeys
Trying
To
Love
While
Hammering
Chain-link fences
Into place
With
Wooden
Spoons

Mission
Accomplishment
By any means
Necessary
Baby
Boo.

# Renaming the Nameless

Touching the
Untouchables
By calling
The Sun
God
Ra
Footzilla?

What the hella?

Well
We ain't
Got much
Else going on—
Might as well
Spice it up
A li'l.

# What Was I Saying Again?

Where does the river flow?
Into other galaxies
Into the system
We know and
Buck
It's just that
Sometimes
We
Forget

I know!
I understand all that!

So
You
Know
They're
Just posers
Putting them-

Selves in
Situations
Over
Us
With
Us
Under
Them?

Yes
But please
Tell me again
How am I on this
Ignorant train of
SsSsSsSsSs*SsSsSsSs*?!?!

Because
You're all
SsSsSsSsSs*SsSsSsSs*!!!!

# Something Else

Kerouac was the old
Kesey was the new
Wolfe had written
Made me regard
Elements in
My own
Specimen

The
Craziness
Of this last
Century

The strife and
Uncertainty
Of all
Ages
To
Come

Pleasant having
Periods
However
Short or
Few
To
Devote
Blessed
Healing
Power
Unto
Yourself
And
You

I've heard
Lonely people
Talking
Texting
Facebooking
Each other
Can make
Each
Other
Lonelier
While
Those free
To do as they
Please often

Dance talk
Imitate
Each
Other—

But then
*I* said
No
Wait
That wasn't it—

# Delightful Transport

Load your dreams
Into a sky car
Gondola
Rise
Above
Climbing
Watching them
Down below mourn
After ya

Good-
Bye
For now

Coming back down
Try not to
Foolishly
Fixate
One
With
Any

Other
Although
Some really
Do deserve it
They also deserve
A fresh
Shot.

# Class, Race, Gender

Break
Binary
Barrier
Banality

Anti-Essentialist
Post-Modernist
Communist
Minimalist
Humanist
Capitalist
Socialist
Gender
Rather
Than
Sex

Fabulous
They scream
They're all

Boring &
Dead—

Whose skin color is next?

Trying to
Shock people
A sure sign you're
Plum green not
Red

Not writing
Not texting
Not speaking
At all
Correct?

Political correcting
Twitter retorts
Are indeed
What's
Next—

Don't be
Surprised
At the
Unrestrained
Greed—
Be shocked
At the

Lack of
Outrage of those
In need

Honest communication
Unfortunately
Is not free.

# The Silky Sledgehammer

Feels so *soft!*
So *smooth!!*
So *right!!!!*

Sledges
Still
Knock
People
Dead
Every
Night
You
Know?

Consider
How little
You actually
Know about this
Lovely lady whose
Hand you're
Holding
Close.

# Movies/Music/Books

Music is probably
The only one
Of
The
Three
I relish
Immensely
With company...

*~Well, usually~*

Movies
For me
Are a bit
More
Solitary...

*~Sometimes, sometimes~*

Books
Most definitely

*~Most nights~*

# On the Verge

⁕

3 ... 2 ... 1...
*Aaaasssss-leeeeep!*

My escape
Planned quickly
One foot slides
Ever so
Unobtrusively
Off the edge
Of the
Bed
When the
Kid says:
Dad—
Pigs don't have
Hair
But
Rabbits can!

Dang
I laughed

He's hilarious &
He's definitely not
Asleep—
Therefore good sir
Resume
Thee position….

Three-year olds
Man
Three-year olds.

# Purple

I like Purple
I want to
Eat
Royal Grapes

Fair enough
Big Girl
I say.

# Regarding the Best

Best Regards
He signs it—
A cliché of a cliché
Even in the corporate
Email business
Charade

I thought
You were cool
Man?

Just sign off
*Best*—
You've obviously
Got it all
Over
The
Rest of us
Lunkheads—

*Later on…*

There he is
Look at his
Homely
Wife attached
To his
Arm—
What a jerk
All decked out
Trying to look like
Some kind of Prince
Charm—

Hey!
Cheers
Mr.—*!*

# Orange & Blue & Gold

Flags
Colors
Banners
Pennants
Materials
Flashing
Catching
Lights
Shining
Certain
Designs
Precise
Seizing
The
Optical eye
And the
One in
The
Mind

Proud of my
Alma Maters

True to my
Schools

Formative
Periods at both
Blue & Gold &
Orange &
Blue.

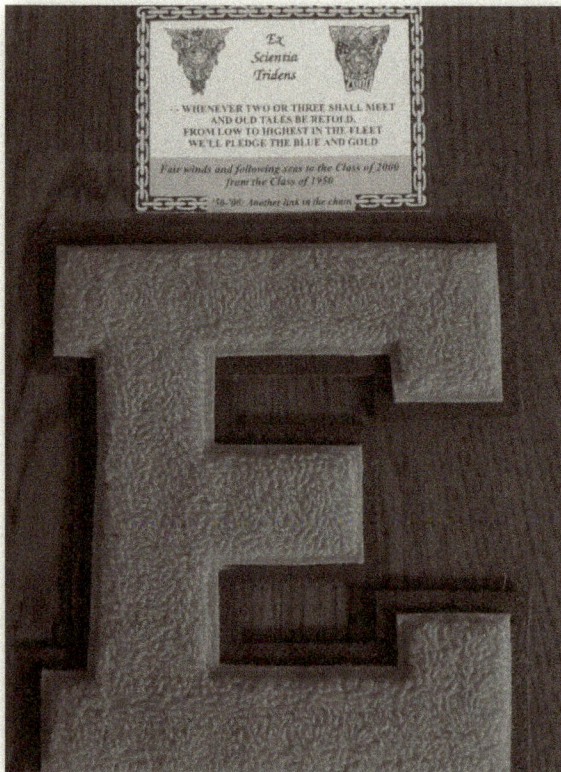

# Reminders

Recall those
Fragrances
Mementoes
Touches
Of
Her
Drifting
Further
Down
The
Stream

Passed
Into
Soaring
Out of history
Coming along
During
Sunny afternoons
Strange interludes
Dead of night

Times of
Delight
Everything
Collapsing
Remerging
Rolling
Right
Along

Why isn't this
Working?

We've found new
Reasons for our
Lack of
Intimacy—

Don't settle my friend

Why put the
Energy
In
If she
Won't be
Genuine?

If it's depleted
What's
The value?

No longer
Where it is
At

Could anything
Bring it
Back?

Would you *want* it back?

Often?
Sometimes?
Only when
Lonely?
Ever?

Have you *never* changed
Your mind?

Talking
Persuading
Hurtling
Myself
Backward
Into a
Time now
Long
Fantasized.

# Ava, What Happened?

My brother glued
Grandma & Grandpa's
Paper to the
Carpet last
Night—

Is this anything important to you?
She asks holding up a
Shredded bank
Statement
To the
Light
With
Objective concern.

I hope not
I say.

Because if it is
It's going to
Look like
This

She holds up
Another shredded piece
This one *more*
Important-looking
Unintelligible
Torn in two
The rest
Glued
To
The
Faux
Turkish rug
Up in the office

How do you know
He did it?

I saw Erich's fingers
Last night
She says
And
They had

Glue
On them.

Hmm.

# Not Quite So Bright

Peace
He said.

Although
He was sharp
He also remembered
A time when he had cracked
Himself up for hours
Searching for a
Fresh garbage bag—
Already took the old
Nasty bag out
Feverishly searching
Throughout the
Garage
Where's that box
Of new
Bags?
Chomping
Hand over
Fist
Only to find

A new bag
Already
Waiting
At the
Bottom
Of the
Can—
Placed
There last
Time so he
Would be prepared
And wouldn't waste any
Time

There went an hour.

People liked to sit and
Watch him challenge
Himself for
Hours

Like the time he committed
To changing the news-
Paper under the
Sink
Every
Month
That nasty
Thin covering
Protecting wood
Underneath from

Chemical
Drippings
Dissolving
Drano
Soaps
Hand
Crèmes of
Various flavors—
He was utterly
Committed until he
Read the date on
The paper there
Under the
Sink
From
The time before:

The South Bend Tribune
Saturday
September 1, 1984.

# Bridge

You're foolish to underestimate
The Power of Passion
She says
Look at the
Gender bridge it gaps—

Life's good with a
Partner
Says her partner
Makes us into better
People

It starts with finding a
Place to cross
The gorge

He
Holds
My pack

I adjust my
Bootstraps

And the
Willingness
To
Get to
The other
Side
He continues

Be advised
She reminds
Me
Ice
Freezes
Quickly
Near the top
If I were you
I might—

I shoulder my pack
Hold up my
Hand

I'll be fine
I say.

# Nuke It

Do it
And be
Done

Stop the threats
If you've got
Cold stones
Drop the
Glowing
Oven
Turn
Us
All
Into
Dust-
Star
Muffins—

World's a POS
Anyway

Haven't stood up for
What's right
Only lain down in the
Face of
Pale
Fear
False
Power
Glowering
Sweeping
Dirt on top
Of our
Beds
While
We're
Out
Sleeping
In the shed

Over and over
Nobody knows how
To kill anymore
Buncha threats
No action

Of course
It's
Different
When you're
Fingering the button

And a
Fraction
Of its
Consequences.

# Persist

Remember when we were
Down and lowly
You said we
Were
Forever?

I never knew
Love had a
Back door

Can't remember to
Forget you

Silent suffering
Boring discussions
Over nothing
(Everything?)
Tends to make
One sore
As
Real
Love

Should
Be beyond
Appearance
Appeal

Ok
I got it
Closed is the
Deal—
Negotiated for more
But there was not
A cent—
No one on
Earth is
Worth
This
Pain
Or
Slit
Wrists
It's my
Life
So I'll
Persist
Continue
Living for
My babies
Who used to
Remind me so
Much of
You.

# It's Been A Year

You should at least
Talk to her or
Something

Everyone
Has
Someone
They don't
Want to see

So we keep busy

How much will you
Claw
Kick
Love
Sacrifice
To be?

What do all
Working

Relationships
Have in
Reality?

Good
Great or
Competent
Communication.

# Blank Page

With
All my
Might I
Focus my
Modus and
Wonder
Do I
Have it
Tonight?

Lighting's
Right
Letters
Symbols
Scribbled
Maximally
Struggling to
Personalize this
Page
Only to discover
My hands

Slayed
Betrayed
Imagination
Frozen on the
Stage

I'm here
Come on
Come *on*
Hurry up
Why is
Is…
Is…
Isn't anything happening?

Laugh?
Take a step
Back?

Oh
Whatever.

# Metaphor

Simile
Says one
Thing's like
Another—

A
Rock
Really is
A word however
A word turned into a
Love-sick
Musical
Refrain
Like some
Annoying mosquito
Buzzing fate into your
Brain
Wanting to
Throw something
Pure cane sugar
Planning something

Charmingly
Wickedly
Worthy
Ends
Up
Alarming
Friends & firemen
Breaking windows
Rushing neighbors
Other good
Folk
Just
Sitting
Down to
Pork chops
Mashed potatoes
Green bean casserole &
Stuffing.

# Rustic Love

Radio
Playing
Richard Marx's
Satisfied while your
Mom said you were
Just getting out
Of the
Shower—

There
You were
Hair wet eyes
Gleaming smiles
Like meteor sunshine
The living room
Lit
Up
As you
And your Mom
Laughed
Hollered

Gave
Each
Other
$#!+

Second Chance
.38 Special
Cheap Trick's
The Flame
Aerosmith
Angel
A
Few
Others
And
Always
Sheriff's
When I'm With You

Fancy seeing you here
My Queen—

You're staying?

Sleep tight
And
Sweet
Dreams.

# Little Words Never Hurt a Good Story

Never be ashamed of a
Lame vocabulary

Don't you tell
Stories every
Day?

What words do
You use or
Create?

You know a few—
Don't hate the language
It becomes an
Ignorant
Fate
Use both sides of
Your brain—
Don't

Abominate
Yourself
Either
Letting
Everyone else
Win

Learn to appreciate
Both angles of
Chagrin.

# I Know You Want It

You want it
Sure
But
Do you
Really
*Deserve*
This instant
Gratification?

Won't be delayed
Although
How's it feel
Afterward
In the
Shade?

Value
Control
Discipline
Dedication
Homemade

# Hello Hi Goodbye

Thanks
For being
You

You helped me heal
I helped you
Along
Too

I've
Been
Hesitant
With this
Broken heart
I know—
Things about
You and me
I love while others
Seem instant
D-day

All I can
Say is
Sorry
But
I
Need
Air for my sails
Wind for my
Flight
After being
Grounded so long
I know we are
Both riding
Smoother lives
Into brighter
Distant
Futures—

Too much?
Too soon?
What's new?

Goodbye honey
I rarely said
I love you
But I
Do.

# Moments of Clarity

When you can see your future
And you don't want it—

What bothers me most is they
Feel they're getting away
With
A
Whole
Charade of
Crimes against
Their own citizens
When no one is
Constantly
Voicing
It
Or
Even
If we are—

These kids we've
Elected to serve us…

We've been served.

# Upon Further Reflection

Experience of age
Hairs of gray
Help
Me
Realize
I was disgusted with
Myself and
Bored

My feelings
Marred

After much
Marinating
Maturation
Please
Accept
My apology.

# Best of It

Best of what's around
Maybe not the most
Tender filet
Soufflé
But
We're
Not just
Seasoning either

You + Me =
Hard to
Believe?

Living a dreamy
Surreal life
Having
Fun
Getting
Stuff done

Ain't perfect—
None of it ever was.

# Forty-One

Forty-one
Runnin'
Along

I
Write
This passage
While still
Forty

A rising crystal ball
Into the
Hall of Gems
1976
November 30th
9:47 p.m.
St. Mary's Hospital
Grand Rapids, Michigan

From that
Anniversary

I write this
Poem
Precisely
Three months
Eleven days
Two hours
Out

Will this be
Just
Another
Year?

Or what it's
All
About?

# Roses are Red?

Roses are red?
Not all are
Red—

Violet's more
Purple than
Blue—

Mon Dieu*!*
Uncouth*!*

How we get
Trapped into
Believing these
Unspeakable
Mistruths*!*

# Liberal Arts

Not yet set in
Stonehenge
Not till you
Sharpen it
Stamp it
Dull it
Your own

Originality's
Always
Alone
Sincerity
Absolutely
Most have
Worked for
What they
Own
Punched the
Timecard

Savvy?
Every
Day
Can't
Forget
That
Because
Life is full of
Dilettantes
Dreamers
Planners
Schemers
Wasters
Drifters
Negative space
Procrastinators
Scam-
Beggar
Artists
Drug-
Damaged
Individuals
Emotional
Dudes and chicks
All with information
For only a few seconds
Of your precious
Precious
Time—

Each second
We give
Essentially
What we're
Reminded
Watching
Cool trickling water
Sinking into
Streams
Thin
Moist
Crevices
Uddered
Up
Dry
Then
Gushing
Trillions of
Tiny water
Crystal stars
Sprinkling
Waterfalls
Glisten
Into the
Light
Blue
Fantastic

A
New
Era

Inheriting
Showers
Absorbing
Love's flowers
Coming back to
Life.

# It's Good

Faced a few fears
Today
Both
Of
Us

Got to play in the dirt
Throw sticks and
Stones in the
Stream
Frogs
&
Turtles
Bopped
-N-
Weaved
With
Nature
So
Many
Soft

Green
Things

Climbed the
Rock wall
Slid down
The Big
Slide

Smile
Buddy
It's okay

It is
A.
O.
K.

# Wandering Riverside

In an aqua-surreal
Blue-moving
Landscape
Entrance
Our shy
Eyes
Led
So easily by
Others who would
So easily lead
Us awry &
Off
Our
Paths of
Bliss

Worried Dictators
Marble-rattled
Whisks
Whipping up
Emotional

Gravitas
Forcing us to
Weather strange moods
Endure hurricane personalities
Climbing out of deep
Wells we never
Want to
Return
To

The
Path
Winds
To the
Right—

Over the river
Across the bridge

The Bridge of
Indifference—

Where I
Leave
These
Feelings
Behind.

# H$_2$O

67%
Incent
Swells
Through
Our cells
As we plead
With ourselves
Never give up in
Our heads or in our
Hearts jesters martyrs
One in all yes giving it
All until the end with
Little stage left
For a third
Verse
$^2/_3$

# X-Mas 2017

Another one
And
Another one
And one more…

Start climbing
Above
The horizon
It's time—
Coming up like
Old Saint
Nicholas
On his
Sleigh
Ride
Leaving
A
Comet
Trail of
Enlightenment

Tis the
Time of the Season

Cheers!

It's Egg Nog—
What?
You don't
Like Holiday
Nog?

# Creatively Distracted

What's the
Plan
To-day
CRK?

Not what
Everyone else
Has planned
Your day
To
Choose
And
Once
Again
You're
Embracing
Entertainment?

I'm talking
Everlasting
Changing
Seasons

Scoring
Soaring
Shots
Of
Golden
Glory
Reborn
Given to
Share
Not late
Swing long
Exploring
Foreign grounds
Middle estates
Not forgetting
To
Touch
Home
Plate—

The Great Great Problem
Of Creation.

# Sharp, Hot, and Vibrating

⤜⟋

Danger: *Razor Sharp!*

H-h-h-*h*-
H-*aaaa*
**Hot!**

Vvv
Vu-Vvvv
vvVuVvVVVVV
Oh! ***Oh Nnoooooooo!***

# Rebooting the Remake

Hardly
An original
Clown anymore
The wrong positions
Same old camera angles
Turbo special effects
Used to
Little effect
Furthering their
Nose and boob jobs
Sexual harassment bobs
By the millions
As people
Watch it
Rake in
Billions—

The top nine say:
Hell yeah baby!
Business trumps labor
Watch our dump

On cable and
In theaters

Then again
This
*Is*
Show
Business

Inequality has always
Existed
This most recent
Boom
Taking off the
Year I was
Born
The Dragon of '76—

CEOs vs.
The Screwed

Still
I remember
When
Going to the
Movies
Was
Cool
Because
The movie was
Good
Too.

# Wonderment

I truly believe
A dog—
Watching
A human
Being
Pull
A
Balloon
Out of
His or her
Pocket
Put it to lips
Blow it up
Tie it off
Toss it
Up
In
The
Air
And

Bop it
Over to a friend—
Must think we're pretty
Godlike.

# Soaring on Two Wings

Everything in life
Changes
Eventually
Hardest stones
Wear their
Wear
Flooded fields
Dry
Dusty
In the air
Clouds disappear

Blue sky
Blessed are we
Who can
Still
Somewhat
Smile
Freely
Deciding
To remove

Our shoes
In mudslide
Rainstorms
Imagining
Warming
The universe
Burning light
To all the
Planets

Life

Who knows
Why
Or
Who?

The only real
Regret lies
Within
You
And
You
Choose
Not to be
Bothered or
Satisfied—

Now fly.

-THE END-

A B O U T   T H E   A U T H O R

⚬

Colin Knapp received his degree in English from the United States Naval Academy in Annapolis. He has studied poetry, acting, prose, and screenwriting. He and his family live in Michigan. *A Chasm Flight* is the first print publication of his poetry. Knapp's next offering, *Tasteful Changes*, will feature two novellas plus a bonus short story to be released as the perfect Halloween treat.
Learn more at: www.colinknapp.com

www.ingramcontent.com/pod-product-compliance
Lightning Source LLC
Chambersburg PA
CBHW031951040426
42448CB00006B/308

* 9 7 8 0 6 9 2 9 9 3 8 1 1 *